**DAILY
KOREAN**

데일리 코리안

1판 1쇄 인쇄   2023. 9. 1.
1판 1쇄 발행   2023. 9. 8.

지은이 피식대학
엮은이 김상엽
영문 감수 허새로미

발행인 고세규
편집 김은하, 김성태 디자인 조명이 마케팅 김새로미 홍보 반재서, 선혜경
발행처 김영사
등록 1979년 5월 17일(제406-2003-036호)
주소 경기도 파주시 문발로 197(문발동) 우편번호 10881
전화 마케팅부 031)955-3100, 편집부 031)955-3200 | 팩스 031)955-3111

값은 뒤표지에 있습니다.
ISBN 978-89-349-4603-8   03190

홈페이지 www.gimmyoung.com   블로그 blog.naver.com/gybook
인스타그램 instagram.com/gimmyoung   이메일 bestbook@gimmyoung.com

좋은 독자가 좋은 책을 만듭니다.
김영사는 독자 여러분의 의견에 항상 귀 기울이고 있습니다.

DAILY
KOREAN

데일리 코리안

피식대학 지음
김상엽 엮음

김영사 × 피식대학 출판부

이 책의 구성과 사용법

- 《데일리 코리안》은 총 4부, 50강의로 이루어져 있습니다.
  Daily Korean covers Part 1-4, 50 lessons.

- 1부 '일상 생활'에서는 다양한 일상 대화에서 사용할 수 있는 기본 표현을 익힙니다.
  Part 1 "Small Talk" gives basic expressions that can be used in a variety of everyday dialogue.

- 2부 '친구 생활'에서는 친구 사이에서 사용할 수 있는 표현을 익힙니다.
  Part 2 "Friendship" gives daily expressions that can be used between friends.

- 3부 '연애 생활'에서는 소개팅 및 데이트 상황, 연인 사이에서 사용할 수 있는 표현을 익힙니다.
  Part 3 "Dating / Romance" gives common expressions that can be used on a blind date or date.

- 4부 '직장 생활'에서는 직장에서 사용할 수 있는 표현을 익힙니다.
  Part 4 "At work" gives expressions that can be used between coworkers.

강의 첫 장 Lesson cover page

강의의 제목. 강의에서 배울
중심 표현을 제시합니다.
Title of the Lesson.
The main expression
of the lesson is explained. ----------

배울 표현의 발음을 설명합니다.
The pronunciation of the expression is
given. ----------------

QR 코드를 통해 유튜브 동영상
강의를 확인할 수 있습니다.
QR codes linked to
the Youtube lecture are given. ----------

활용해 봅시다 Let's put it to use

대화문 예시입니다.
살아 있는 표현들이므로 실생활에서
유용하게 사용할 수 있습니다.
Sample dialogue. These examples are
useful in everyday life.

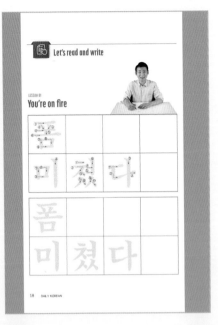

읽고 써봅시다 Let's read and write

강의에서 배운 표현을 직접 반복해 쓰면서 연습할 수 있습니다.

This exercise links writing with reading. Students can practice writing the expression repeatedly they have just learned.

상황을 만들어봅시다
Let's make your situation

강의에서 배운 표현을 추가로 연습해 볼 수 있습니다. 각 표현은 다양한 상황에서 활용될 수 있습니다.

Suggestions for further practice are given. The expressions can be adapted to various situations.

한국 문화 배우기 | Korean Culture Tips

한국의 문화를 소개합니다.

한국의 상황별 문화와 예절을 학습할 수 있습니다.

An aspect of Korean culture is introduced.

Students can learn about Korean culture and proper manners in a certain situation.

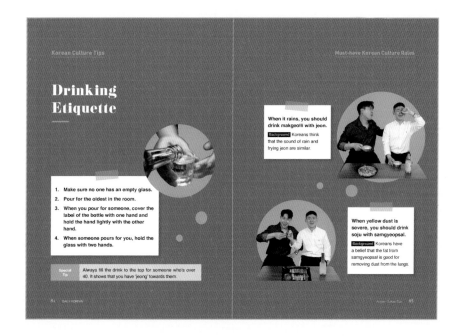

심화 표현: 어두와 어미 Advanced Expressions: prefixes & suffixes

최신 유행하는 한국어 어두, 어미 표현을 소개합니다.

Up-to-date Korean prefixes and suffixes are given.

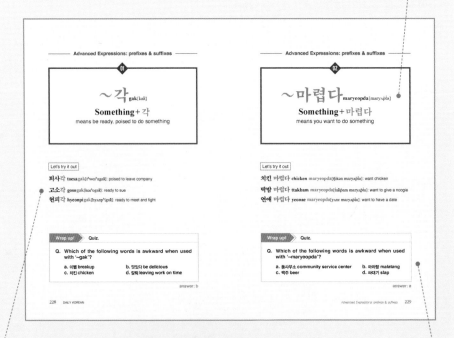

각 표현의 활용 예시와 용법(의미)을 학습합니다.

Explanations of the usage(meaning) and examples are given.

간단한 테스트를 통해 해당 표현의 이해도를 점검할 수 있습니다.

These questions test the students' understanding of the expression.

모바일 축약어 Texting & Chatting Abbreviations

휴대전화 메시지나 온라인 채팅 상황에서 사용할 수 있는 유용한 축약어를 소개합니다.
Useful abbreviations to use in text messages or online chat situations are introduced.

Texting & Chatting Abbreviations

In English	In Korean
Let's do it	ㄱㄱ
Yes	ㅇㅇ
No	ㄴㄴ
LOL	ㅋㅋ
Get out of	ㄲㅈ
Nope	ㅅㄹ
Where are you	ㅇㄷ
Shut up	ㄷㅊ
Really?	ㄹㅇ?
Hi	ㅎㅇ
Bye	ㅃㅇ

Texting & Chatting Abbreviations

In English	In Korean
OMG…	ㄷㄷ
Tsk tsk	ㅉㅉ
Just wait	ㄱㄷ
Bye, keep working	ㅅㄱ
I'm sorry	ㅈㅅ
I agree	ㅇㅈ
Oh yeah!	ㄱㅇㄷ
Haha	ㅎㅎ
Thank you	ㄱㅅ
I don't know	ㅁㄹ
Congrat!	ㅊㅋ

C O N T E N T S

Part 2 FRIENDSHIP 친구 생활

C O N T E N T S

Part 3   DATING/ROMANCE 연애 생활

Part 4   AT WORK 직장 생활

Part 1

SMALL TALK
일상 생활

01
LESSON

You're on fire

폼 미쳤다

pom   michyeotda

[pʰom mitsʰʌ́tt͡a]

피식대학 유튜브 채널에서 강의 영상을 확인하세요.
Please check the video of the lecture on our
YouTube channel of Psick University.

Daniel   야, 민수야.
Hey, Kenneth!

Kenneth   용주 형, 무슨 일이야?
What's up Daniel?

Daniel   너 어제 쏘니 게임 봤어?
Did you watch Heung-min Son's game last night?

Kenneth   응, 봤어.
Yes, of course.

Daniel   쏘니 폼 미쳤다.
Sonny was on fire!

Kenneth   쏘니 폼 미쳤다?
Sonny was on fire?

Daniel   쏘니 폼 미쳤다!
Sonny's pom michyeotda!

Let's read and write

LESSON 01
You're on fire

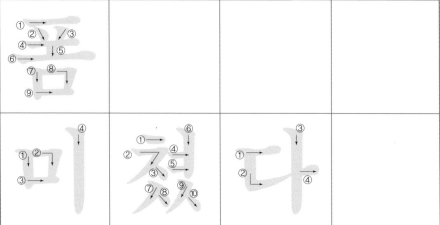

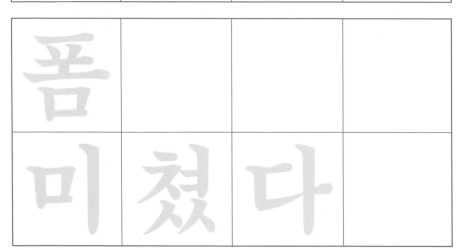

폼		미	쳤	다	
폼		미	쳤	다	
폼		미	쳤	다	
폼		미	쳤	다	
폼		미	쳤	다	
폼		미	쳤	다	
폼		미	쳤	다	

Let's take a break

담타
damta

[tamtʰa]

피식대학 유튜브 채널에서 강의 영상을 확인하세요.
Please check the video of the lecture on our
YouTube channel of Psick University.

Kenneth 그건 내일까지 보내드리겠습니다.
Alright, I will send it by tomorrow.

Daniel 야, 김 대리.
Hey, Kenneth!

Kenneth 어, 부장님!
Oh, Daniel···

Daniel 여태까지 일한 거야?
You've been working til now?

Kenneth 그렇습니다.
Yes···

Daniel 자네 정말 이달의 우수 사원이야.
You're the best employee of the month.

Kenneth 감사합니다.
Thank you.

Daniel 그러지 말고 담타?
Do you want damta?

Kenneth 담타?!
Little break?

Daniel 우리 잠깐 담타!
Let's take a break!

Let's read and write

Let's take a break

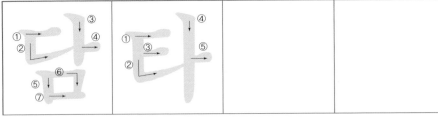

Let's make your situation

I'm so nervous

똥줄 탄다

ttongjul　　　　tanda

[t̬oŋdzul tʰanda]

피식대학 유튜브 채널에서 강의 영상을 확인하세요.

Please check the video of the lecture on our
YouTube channel of Psick University.

Daniel 야, 민수야, 너 무슨 일 있어?
Hey Kenneth, is everything okay?

Kenneth 나 마고 로비랑 사귀는 거 알잖아.
You know, I am dating Margot Robbie.

Daniel 그렇지.
Yeah, I know that.

Kenneth 근데 캔들 제너랑 바람피우는 거 마고 로비가 알아버렸어.
But I got caught cheating with Kendall Jenner.

Daniel 와… 그럼 너 두 명 만나는 거야?
Wow… so are you dating two people?

Kenneth 아니, 다섯 명…
No, five…

Daniel 어우… 너 괜찮아?
Dang… are you okay?

Kenneth 아니, 나 똥줄 탄다.
No, I am ttongjul tanda.

Daniel 너 똥줄 탄다?
Are you nervous?

Kenneth 응, 나 똥줄 탄다.
Yeah, I am ttongjul tanda.

K&D 민수는 똥줄 탄다.
Kenneth is nervous.

Let's read and write

LESSON 03

I'm so nervous

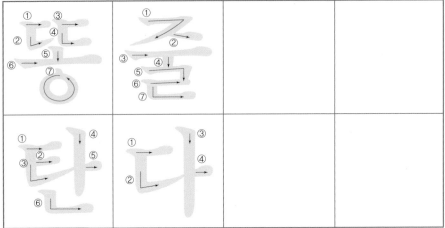

똥	줄		탄	다	
똥	줄		탄	다	
똥	줄		탄	다	
똥	줄		탄	다	
똥	줄		탄	다	
똥	줄		탄	다	
똥	줄		탄	다	

Do your best

빼끼 치지 마
ppaengkki　　chiji　　ma

[pɛŋk͈i tsʰidzi ma]

피식대학 유튜브 채널에서 강의 영상을 확인하세요.
Please check the video of the lecture on our
YouTube channel of Psick University.

Let's put it to use

Daniel	야 민수야, 너 왜 이렇게 못 놀아? Hey Kenneth, are you bored or something?
Kenneth	나 힘들어. I'm tired.
Daniel	그래도 여기까지 왔는데, 열심히 놀아야지. Dude, we came all the way here. Let's have some fun.
Kenneth	아, 피곤해. I'm exhausted.
Daniel	그러지 말고 놀자. Come on, let's go hard.
Kenneth	됐어, 어차피 티 안 나. It doesn't matter.
Superstar	야, 뺑끼 치지 마. Hey, ppaengkki chiji ma.
K&D	뺑끼 치지 마? Don't be lazy?
Superstar	뺑끼 치지 마! Do your best!
K&D	뺑끼 치지 마? Just enjoy the party?
K&D	우리 뺑끼 치지 마! We should do our best!

LESSON 04
Do your best

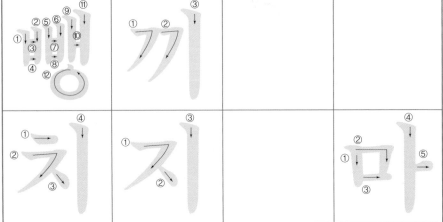

빵	끼		치	지	
마					

빵	끼		치	지	
마					

빵	끼		치	지	
마					

빵	끼		치	지	
마					

05
LESSON

It's mine

떱

ttip

[t̀ip]

 피식대학 유튜브 채널에서 강의 영상을 확인하세요.
Please check the video of the lecture on our
YouTube channel of Psick University.

Let's put it to use

(냠냠 쩝쩝 Yum yum)

Daniel 여기 떡볶이 진짜 맛있다.
This tteokbokki is so good.

Kenneth 어… 이제 하나 남았네…
Oh… only one left…

(…)

K&D 띱!
Ttip!

K&D 띱!
It's mine!

K&D 띱!!!!
Don't touch it!! It's mine!!!

LESSON 05
It's mine

Let's make your situation

I gotta go

엄크 떴다

eomkeu   tteotda

[ʌmkʰɯ t͈ʌt͈a]

피식대학 유튜브 채널에서 강의 영상을 확인하세요.(추후 업로드 예정)
Please check the video of the lecture on our
YouTube channel of Psick University.(Uploading soon)

Let's put it to use

(디스코드 하는 상황 Playing online game)

Kenneth 새벽에 게임 하니까 더 재밌다. 그치, 용주 형.
Playing games at night is the best!

Daniel ⋯

Kenneth 용주 형?
Daniel?

Daniel ⋯

Kenneth 왔다!! 빨리 공격해!! 아, 뭐 해, 죽었잖아.
Yo! Go get em! Ahh man. What are you doing?

Daniel ⋯아 나 엄크 떴다.
Eomkeu tteotda.

Kenneth 엄크 떴어?
You gotta go?

Daniel 엄크 떴어⋯
I gotta go⋯

K&D 용주 형은 엄크 떴어.
Daniel gotta go⋯

Daniel 내일 다시 하자.
Let's play tomorrow.

(로그아웃 Log out)

Let's read and write

LESSON 06
I gotta go

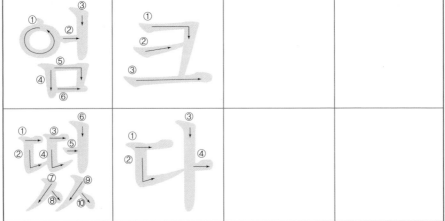

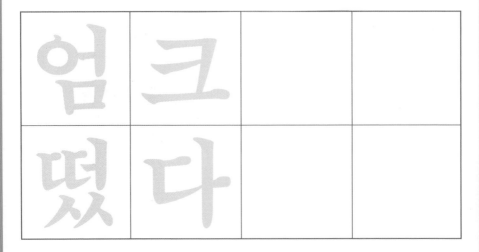

엄	크		떴	다	
엄	크		떴	다	
엄	크		떴	다	
엄	크		떴	다	
엄	크		떴	다	
엄	크		떴	다	
엄	크		떴	다	

Can you please stop doing that?

방을 잡아라

bangeul   jabara

[paŋul tsabara]

피식대학 유튜브 채널에서 강의 영상을 확인하세요.
Please check the video of the lecture on our
YouTube channel of Psick University.

(공공장소에서 키스하는 커플 A couple kissing in public)

Kenneth 뭔 소리야?

What's this noise?

Kenneth 헉, 용주 형. 저기 봐봐.

OMG, Daniel⋯ look over there.

Daniel 오⋯ 나 어렸을 땐, 누가 보면 어떡할까 걱정했는데, 요즘 애들은 꼭 보라고 저러는 거 같아.

I was worried about other people seeing me. But these days, they act as if they want to be seen.

Kenneth 방을 잡아라.

Bangeul jabara.

Daniel 방을 잡아라.

Please stop it.

K&D 제발 방을 잡아라!

Can you please stop doing that?

Let's read and write

Can you please stop doing that?

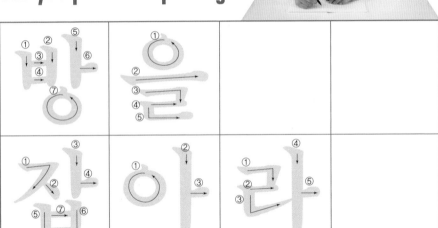

방	을		잡	아	라
방	을		잡	아	라
방	을		잡	아	라
방	을		잡	아	라
방	을		잡	아	라
방	을		잡	아	라
방	을		잡	아	라

08
LESSON

Please stop me
야, 말리지 마

ya   malliji   ma

[ya maʎʎidzi ma]

피식대학 유튜브 채널에서 강의 영상을 확인하세요.(추후 업로드 예정)
Please check the video of the lecture on our
YouTube channel of Psick University.(Uploading soon)

Kenneth 저기 문신 돼지 좀 봐봐, 진짜 꼴 보기 싫다.
Hey, look at that man. He's a tattooed pig, it is a real eyesore!

Daniel 야 그만해, 들어.
Hey stop it, he can hear you···

Jaehyung 삼촌, 뭐라 했습니까?
Hey, what did you say?

Kenneth 아무 말도 안 했는데요.
I didn't say anything.

Jaehyung 뭐라 했잖아. 쥐방울만 한 놈아.
Don't mess with me, you little sh*t.

Kenneth 뭐 쥐방울?! 뚜껑 열리네. 야, 말리지 마.
What the? I'm so pissed off. Ya malliji ma.

Daniel 그만해, 좀.
Please don't do that.

Kenneth 야, 말리지 말라고.
Please stop me.

Daniel 너 그러다 큰일 나.
You're going to be in big trouble.

Kenneth 말리지 말라고···!
Please! Stop me!!

Let's read and write

Please stop me

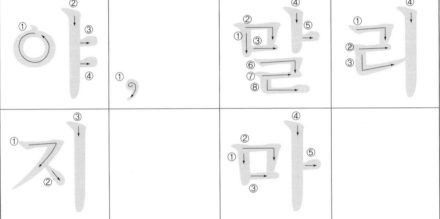

야	,	말	리	지	
마					

야	,	말	리	지	
마					

야	,	말	리	지	
마					

야	,	말	리	지	
마					

09
LESSON

Are you sure?

다 걸고?
da   geolgo

[ta kʌlgo]

피식대학 유튜브 채널에서 강의 영상을 확인하세요.(추후 업로드 예정)
Please check the video of the lecture on our
YouTube channel of Psick University.(Uploading soon)

Let's put it to use

Daniel 야, 민수야.
Hey, Kenneth.

Kenneth 어, 용주 형!
Oh, Daniel!

Daniel 이번에 피식 쇼에 손흥민 나온대.
Sonny is coming on Psick Show.

Kenneth 에이, 뻥 치지 마.
Do not lie.

Daniel 내가 거짓말을 왜 해?
Why would I lie to you?

Kenneth 다 걸고?
Da geolgo?

Daniel 진짜라니까!
Come on, this is true! I swear!

Kenneth 다 걸고?
Are you sure?

Daniel 진짜로 다 걸고!
Obviously, I am sure!

Let's read and write

LESSON 09
Are you sure?

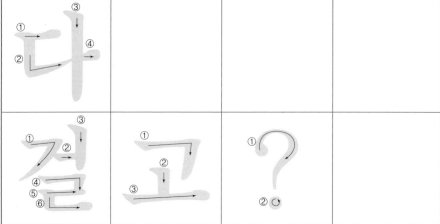

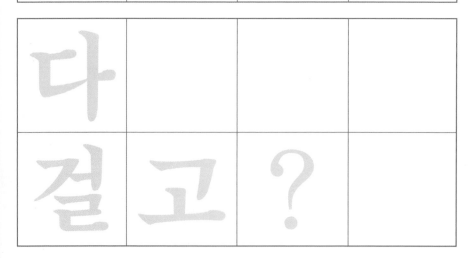

다		걸	고	?	

다		걸	고	?	

다		걸	고	?	

다		걸	고	?	

다		걸	고	?	

다		걸	고	?	

다		걸	고	?	

Please, be quiet

전세 냈어?

jeonse   naesseo

[tsʌnsʰe nɛɕʌ]

피식대학 유튜브 채널에서 강의 영상을 확인하세요.
Please check the video of the lecture on our
YouTube channel of Psick University.

Let's put it to use

Daniel (통화 중) 어, 민수야! 나 한국 왔어. 그래, 빨리 와…
(On the phone) Hey, I just landed. Yes, come pick me u…

Kenneth (툭툭) 모두가 쓰는 공간입니다.
(Knock knock) Excuse me. This is a public space.

Daniel 아 예… 예…
Ah, okay I got it.

Daniel 아니, 나 오랜만에 한국 왔는데 잠깐…
Come on man. It's been a while I visited Korea. Hurry up…

Kenneth (툭툭) 사람들이 많습니다.
(Knock knock) There are so many people around you…

Daniel 아, 예. 민수야, 일단 나오라니까.
Okay, I got it. No, it's nothing, just hurry up and pick me up man.

Kenneth (툭툭)
(Knock knock)

Daniel 뭐요?
What?

Kenneth 이 양반아, 지하철 전세 냈어?
Hey mister, you are jeonse naesseo on this subway?

Daniel 전세 냈어?
Was I too loud?

Kenneth 전세 냈어?!
Yes, please be quiet!

Let's read and write

Please, be quiet

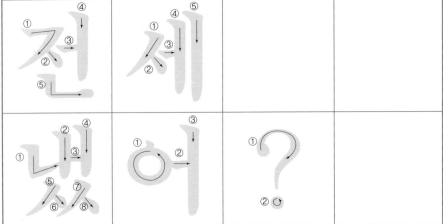

전	세		냈	어	?
전	세		냈	어	?
전	세		냈	어	?
전	세		냈	어	?
전	세		냈	어	?
전	세		냈	어	?
전	세		냈	어	?

Never give up

중꺽마

jungkkeongma

[tsuŋkʌŋma]

피식대학 유튜브 채널에서 강의 영상을 확인하세요.
Please check the video of the lecture on our
YouTube channel of Psick University.

Daniel	야 민수야, 너 얼굴이 왜 그래?
	Hey Kenneth, why the long face?
Kenneth	나 사실은 섯다 치다가 집문서 날리고 땅문서 날리고 다 잃었어…
	Well… actually, I lost everything to gambling.
Daniel	이야… 너 괜찮아?
	Man… are you okay?
Kenneth	아니, 나 그냥 모든 걸 포기할래.
	No… I just want to give up everything.
Daniel	민수야, 중꺾마.
	Hey Kenneth, jungkkeongma.
Kenneth	중꺾마?
	Never give up?
Daniel	중꺾마!
	Never give up!
K&D	중요한 건 꺾이지 않는 마음!
	Jungyohan geon kkeokkiji anneun maeum!

Let's read and write

Never give up

중꺾마

중꺾마

중꺾마

중	꺾	마			
중	꺾	마			
중	꺾	마			
중	꺾	마			
중	꺾	마			
중	꺾	마			
중	꺾	마			

12
LESSON

Can I get a discount?

현금으로
hyeongeumeuro

할 건데
hal   geonde

[hyʌngɯmɯro hal kʼʌnde]

피식대학 유튜브 채널에서 강의 영상을 확인하세요.
Please check the video of the lecture on our
YouTube channel of Psick University.

Daniel 오이소, 보이소, 사이소!
Come, take a look! Everything's on sale!

Kenneth 저기, 사장님.
Hi.

Daniel 오이소.
Welcome!

Kenneth 이거 얼마예요?
How much is this?

Daniel 이거 6만 원.
This is 60 bucks.

Kenneth 6만 원? 너무 비싸다!
60 bucks? Too expensive!

Daniel 원가. 남는 거 없어요.
No margin… I'm losing money at this price.

Kenneth 나 현금으로 할 건데.
Actually, I will hyeongeumeuro hal geonde.

Daniel 현금으로 할 건데?
Are you going to pay in cash?

Kenneth 현금으로 할 건데!
Can I get a discount, please?

Let's read and write

LESSON 12
Can I get a discount?

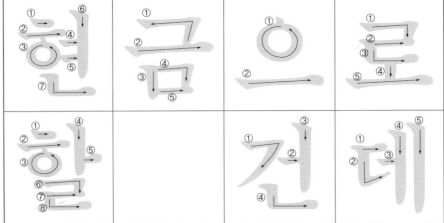

현	금	으	로		할
건	데				

현	금	으	로		할
건	데				

현	금	으	로		할
건	데				

현	금	으	로		할
건	데				

It's not my style

돌아보고
dorabogo

올게요
olgeyo

[torabogo olk'eyo]

피식대학 유튜브 채널에서 강의 영상을 확인하세요.
Please check the video of the lecture on our
YouTube channel of Psick University.

Daniel 와, 이거 완전 손님 거다.
Oh my, this clothing is yours.

Kenneth 아… 전 잘 모르겠는데…
Well… I'm not sure.

Daniel 이거 그냥 입고 가요.
Just take this. It's yours.

Daniel 현금으로 하면 더 싸게 해드릴게.
If you pay in cash, I'll give you a discount.

Kenneth 저기요, 저 돌아보고 올게요.
I will dorabogo olgeyo!

Daniel 돌아보고 올게요?
You think it's not your style?

Kenneth 돌아보고 올게요!
I will take a look around.

Daniel 돌아보고 올게요?
You really don't like it?

Kenneth 저 돌아보고 올게요!
I'm sorry, it's not my style!

Let's read and write

LESSON 13

It's not my style

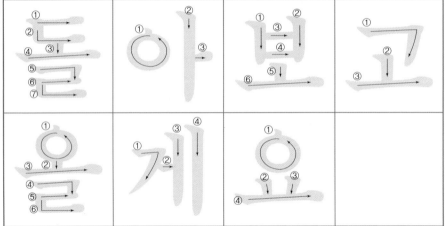

돌	아	보	고		올
게	요				

돌	아	보	고		올
게	요				

돌	아	보	고		올
게	요				

돌	아	보	고		올
게	요				

I don't like your service

사장 나오라
sajang   naora

그래
geurae

[sʰadzaŋ naora kɯrɛ]

피식대학 유튜브 채널에서 강의 영상을 확인하세요.(추후 업로드 예정)
Please check the video of the lecture on our
YouTube channel of Psick University.(Uploading soon)

Kenneth 저기요, 여기 물 좀 더 주세요.
Excuse me. Can I have some water?

Daniel (···툭)
(Putting a cup down with a thud)

Daniel 뭐야, 왜 이렇게 불친절해···
What the hell. They are so rude.

Kenneth 저기요, 여기 김치도 좀 더 주세요.
Excuse me. Can I also have some more kimchi?

Daniel (툭)
(Putting a dish down with a thud)

Kenneth 하··· 저기요, 사장 나오라 그래.
Hmm··· hey, sajang naora geurae.

Daniel 왜요?
Why?

Kenneth 사장 나오라 그래.
I don't like your service.

Daniel 난 잘못한 게 없어요.
I didn't do anything wrong.

Kenneth 알겠으니까,
사장 나오라 그래!
I just, I don't like your service!

Let's read and write

I don't like your service

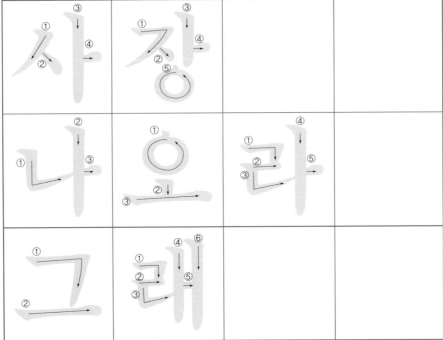

사	장		나	오	라
그	래				

사	장		나	오	라
그	래				

사	장		나	오	라
그	래				

사	장		나	오	라
그	래				

Is this you?

당근이세요?

danggeuniseyo

[taŋɡɯɲisʰeyo]

피식대학 유튜브 채널에서 강의 영상을 확인하세요.(추후 업로드 예정)
Please check the video of the lecture on our
YouTube channel of Psick University.(Uploading soon)

(중고 거래자 찾는 중 Looking for the secondhand dealer supposed to meet up on Craigslist)

Kenneth   (두리번두리번) **여기가 맞는데, 어딨는 거야?**
(Looking around) Must be here··· where is he?

Kenneth   (두리번두리번) **아, 저 사람인가?**
(Looking around) Oh, is that him?

Kenneth   **저기요, 혹시 당근이세요?**
Excuse me. Danggeuniseyo?

Daniel   **네?**
Sorry?

Kenneth   **당근이세요?**
Is this you?

Daniel   **네?**
Huh?

Kenneth   **당근이세요?!**
You are the guy, right?

Daniel   **저 아닌데요.**
No, it's not me.

Kenneth   **아, 죄송합니다···**
진짜 어딨는 거야··· 흑흑.
Oh my bad.
Where the hell is he···

Let's read and write

Is this you?

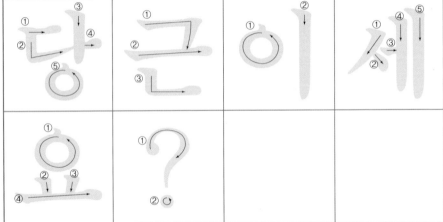

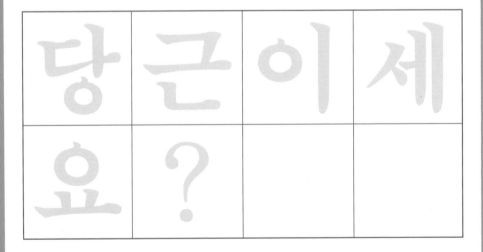

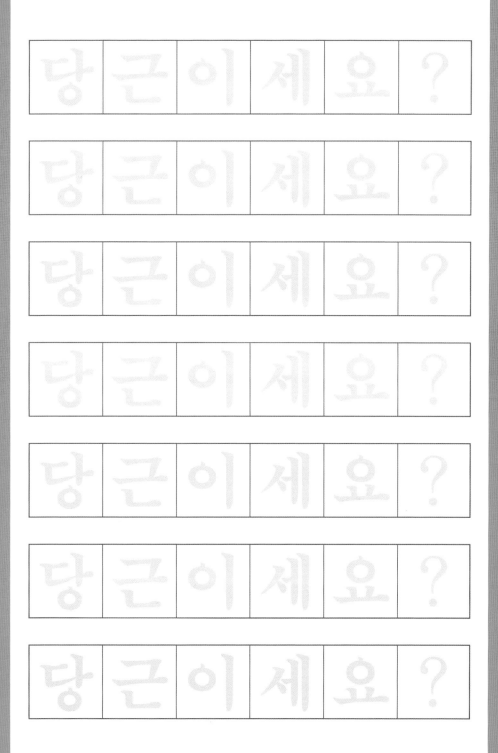

당	근	이	세	요	?
당	근	이	세	요	?
당	근	이	세	요	?
당	근	이	세	요	?
당	근	이	세	요	?
당	근	이	세	요	?
당	근	이	세	요	?

This is extremely hot

신라면 정도예요

sillamyeon   jeongdoyeyo

[çillamyʌn tsʌŋdoyeyo]

피식대학 유튜브 채널에서 강의 영상을 확인하세요.
Please check the video of the lecture on our
YouTube channel of Psick University.

Kenneth   저기요, 주문할게요.
Can I order?

Daniel   네, 어떤 걸로 준비해 드릴까요?
Sure, what can I get you?

Kenneth   김치찌개 이거 얼마나 매워요?
How spicy is this kimchi soup?

Daniel   많이 매워요.
This is really spicy.

Kenneth   그래서, 얼마나 매워요?
So how spicy is this?

Daniel   신라면 정도예요.
This is sillamyeon jeongdoyeyo.

Kenneth   아, 신라면 정도예요?
Oh, this is extremely hot!

Daniel   신라면 정도예요!
Yeah, this is extremely hot!

K&D   이 김치찌개는
신라면 정도예요!
This kimchi soup is
extremely hot!!

Let's read and write

This is extremely hot

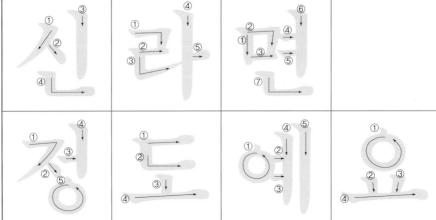

신	라	면		정	도
예	요				

신	라	면		정	도
예	요				

신	라	면		정	도
예	요				

신	라	면		정	도
예	요				

Make some noise

소리 벗고
sori   beotgo

팬티 질러
paenti   jilleo

[sʰori pʌtk̚o pʰentʰi tsillʌ]

피식대학 유튜브 채널에서 강의 영상을 확인하세요.
Please check the video of the lecture on our
YouTube channel of Psick University.

Let's put it to use

Superstar   무대가 뜨거워요!
This stage is hot!

K&D   예!!
Yeah!!

Superstar   잔치 준비 됐나요?
Y'all ready to party?

K&D   예!!
Yeah!!

Superstar   소리 벗고 팬티 질러!
Sori beotgo paenti jilleo!!

K&D   소리 벗고 팬티 질러!!
Sori beotgo paenti jilleo!!

Superstar   소리 벗고 팬티 질러!
Make some noise!

K&D   소리 벗고 팬티 질러!!
Make some noise!!!

Let's read and write

LESSON 17
Make some noise

소	리		
벗	고		
팬	티		
질	러		

소	리		벗	고	
팬	티		질	러	

소	리		벗	고	
팬	티		질	러	

소	리		벗	고	
팬	티		질	러	

소	리		벗	고	
팬	티		질	러	

Drinking Etiquette

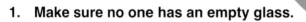

1. Make sure no one has an empty glass.

2. Pour for the oldest in the room.

3. When you pour for someone, cover the label of the bottle with one hand and hold the hand lightly with the other hand.

4. When someone pours for you, hold the glass with two hands.

Special Tip	Always fill the drink to the top for someone who's over 40. It shows that you have 'jeong' towards them.

When it rains, you should drink makgeolli with jeon.

Background Koreans think that the sound of rain and frying jeon are similar.

When yellow dust is severe, you should drink soju with samgyeopsal.

Background Koreans have a belief that the fat from samgyeopsal is good for removing dust from the lungs.

Part 2

FRIENDSHIP

친구 생활

Crush on you

여기 재미없죠?

yeogi   jaemieopjyo

[jʌgi dʑɛmiʌptɕ̚jo]

피식대학 유튜브 채널에서 강의 영상을 확인하세요.
Please check the video of the lecture on our
YouTube channel of Psick University.

(클럽 안 상황 In a Club)

Kenneth 저기요, 몇 살이에요?
Hey, excuse me. Can I ask how old you are?

Daisy 저 스무 살이요.
I'm 20 years old.

Kenneth 되게 동안이다. 스물한 살인 줄 알았는데.
You look so young. I thought you were 21.

Daisy 꺄르륵
lol

Kenneth 근데, 여기 재미없죠?
By the way, yeogi jaemieopjyo?

Daisy 뭐라고요?
What did you say?

Kenneth 여기 재미없죠?
I have a crush on you.

Daisy 뭐라고요?
I can't hear you.

Kenneth 여기 재미없죠?!
I've a crush on you!

Daisy 밖에서 봐요.
Okay, see you outside.

Let's read and write

LESSON 18
Crush on you

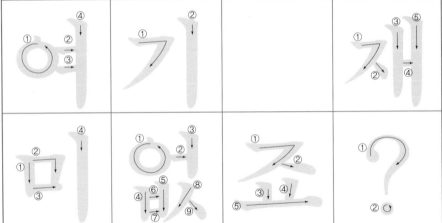

여	기		재	미	없
죠	?				

여	기		재	미	없
죠	?				

여	기		재	미	없
죠	?				

여	기		재	미	없
죠	?				

19
LESSON

He's not attractive

니 남친
ni   namchin

지나간다
jinaganda

[ni namtsʰin tsinaganda]

 피식대학 유튜브 채널에서 강의 영상을 확인하세요.
Please check the video of the lecture on our
YouTube channel of Psick University.

Let's put it to use

Katherine 어머, 용숙아.
Hey, Daisy.

Daisy 야, 민순아!
What's up, Katherine.

Katherine 너 진짜 예뻐졌다.
What happened to you, girl.

Daisy 너 몸매 대박이야.
You look dang good.

Katherine 니가 더 예뻐.
Oh, shut up. You look better.

Daisy 에이⋯
Nah⋯

(남자가 지나간다. A dude passes by.)

Katherine 저기, 니 남친 지나간다.
Hey, ni namchin jinaganda.

Daisy 뭐라고?
What did you say?

Katherine 니 남친 지나간다.
Isn't he your boyfriend?

Daisy 너 말 다 했어?
How are you!

Katherine 저기, 니 남친 지나간다!
He's not attractive.

Let's read and write

He's not attractive

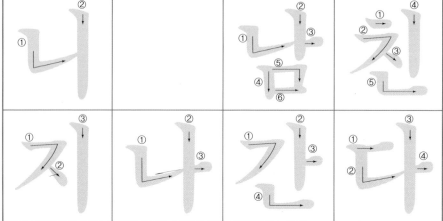

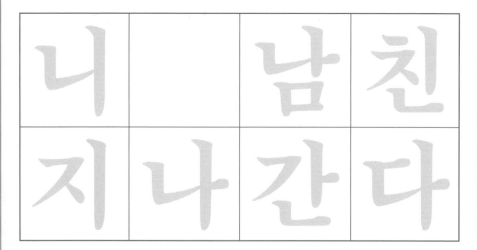

니		남	친		지
나	간	다			

니		남	친		지
나	간	다			

니		남	친		지
나	간	다			

니		남	친		지
나	간	다			

20
LESSON

What's wrong with you?

너 T야?

neo   tiya

[nʌ tʰiya]

 피식대학 유튜브 채널에서 강의 영상을 확인하세요.
Please check the video of the lecture on our
YouTube channel of Psick University.

Kenneth 용주 형, 나 걔랑 헤어졌어. 흑흑.
Daniel, I··· broke up with her.

Daniel 그냥 다른 여자 만나.
Just meet another girl.

Kenneth 뭐··· 뭐라고?
What··· what did you say?

Daniel 아니, 다른 여자 만나라고.
I said, just meet another girl.

Kenneth 너 T야?
Neo tiya?

Daniel 아니 뭐가 문제야, 다른 여자 많은데.
Hey, what is the problem? There are so many other girls.

Kenneth X발 너 T야?
Ssibal neo tiya?

Daniel 아니, 다른 여자 많은데 왜 그러는 거야.
Come on, look, you could have anyone you want.

Kenneth T발 너 C야?
Tibal neo ssiya?

Daniel 아니 왜 욕을 해, 다른 여자 만나면 되지.
Don't curse at me. Just meet another girl.

Kenneth 용주 형은 X발 T야.
Daniel, Fxxk off, what's wrong with you?

Daniel 민수는 X발 F야.
You're so emotional.

Let's read and write

LESSON 20

What's wrong with you?

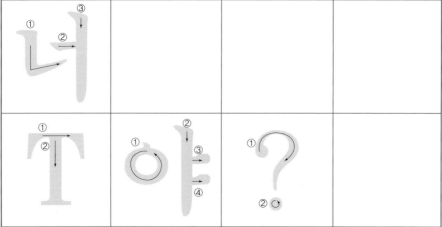

너		ㅜ	야	?	

너		ㅜ	야	?	

너		ㅜ	야	?	

너		ㅜ	야	?	

너		ㅜ	야	?	

너		ㅜ	야	?	

너		ㅜ	야	?	

21
LESSON

You want a piece of me?

너 뭐 돼?

neo   mwo   dwae

[nʌ mwʌ twɛ]

 피식대학 유튜브 채널에서 강의 영상을 확인하세요.
Please check the video of the lecture on our
YouTube channel of Psick University.

Let's put it to use

Kenneth 저기요, 어깨를 쳤으면 사과를 해야죠.
Come on man, you don't even say sorry for shoulder checking me?

Daniel 야, 방구 낀 놈이 성낸다더니, 어디서 적반하장이야.
Hey, little boy, you are the one who shoulder checked me!

Kenneth 왜 반말해?
Why you talk to me like that?

Daniel 내 맘이야.
Because I can.

Kenneth 너 뭐 돼?
Neo mwo dwae?

Daniel 뭐라고?
What?

Kenneth 너 뭐 돼?
You want a piece of me?

Daniel 너 뭐라고 했어?
What did you say?

Kenneth 너 뭐 돼?!
You want a piece of me?!

Daniel 너, 따라 나와.
Catch me outside.

LESSON 21
You want a piece of me?

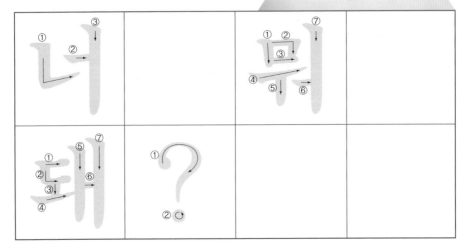

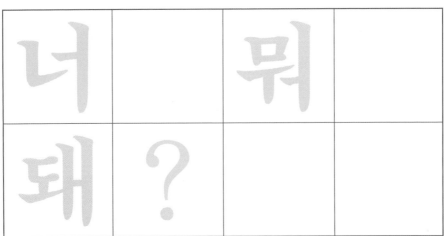

너		뭐		돼	?

너		뭐		돼	?

너		뭐		돼	?

너		뭐		돼	?

너		뭐		돼	?

너		뭐		돼	?

너		뭐		돼	?

You have a terrible taste

돈 주고 샀어?

don   jugo   sasseo

[ton tsugo sʰaśʌ]

피식대학 유튜브 채널에서 강의 영상을 확인하세요. (추후 업로드 예정)
Please check the video of the lecture on our
YouTube channel of Psick University.(Uploading soon)

Let's put it to use

Kenneth 용주 형!
Daniel!

Daniel 어, 민수야!
Yo, Kenneth!

Kenneth 나 오늘 어때?
How do I look today?

Daniel 그 옷은 뭐야…?
What the hell is that?

Kenneth 예쁘지? 이번에 새로 나온 신상이야.
Isn't it fire? It's from the new collection!

Daniel 돈 주고 샀어?
Don jugo sasseo?

Kenneth 응, 12개월 할부로 바로 긁었어.
Yeah, I bought it on 12 months installment.

Daniel 돈 주고 샀어??
You have a terrible taste.

Kenneth 응, 부러우면 빌려줄까?
I can lend it to you if you want.

Daniel 돈 주고 샀어?
You have a terrible taste!

Let's read and write

LESSON 22
You have a terrible taste

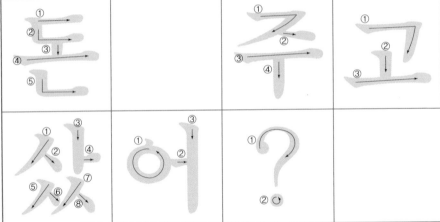

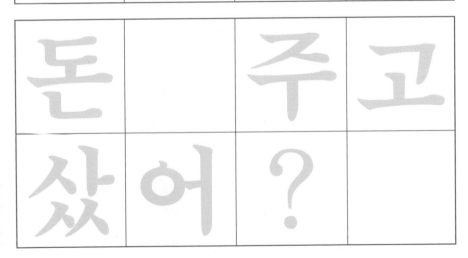

돈		주	고		샀
어	?				

돈		주	고		샀
어	?				

돈		주	고		샀
어	?				

돈		주	고		샀
어	?				

I'll be late

출발했어

chulbalhaesseo

[tsʰulbalhɛ́s̓ʌ]

피식대학 유튜브 채널에서 강의 영상을 확인하세요.
Please check the video of the lecture on our
YouTube channel of Psick University.

Let's put it to use

(따르르릉, 따르르릉 RRRRR, RRRRR)

Daniel 아뿔싸! (통화 중) 어, 민수야.
Oh my gosh. (On the phone) Oh, hello Kenneth.

Kenneth 어 용주 형, 오고 있지?
Hello Daniel, you're on your way right?

Daniel 어, 나 출발했어.
Uh, yes… I'm chulbalhaesseo.

Kenneth 지금 일어났어?
Did you just wake up?

Daniel 아니, 출발했어!
No, I'm on my way.

Kenneth 지금 일어났네!
Come on, you just woke up.

Daniel 나는 출발했어!
Actually, I'll be late…

LESSON 23
I'll be late

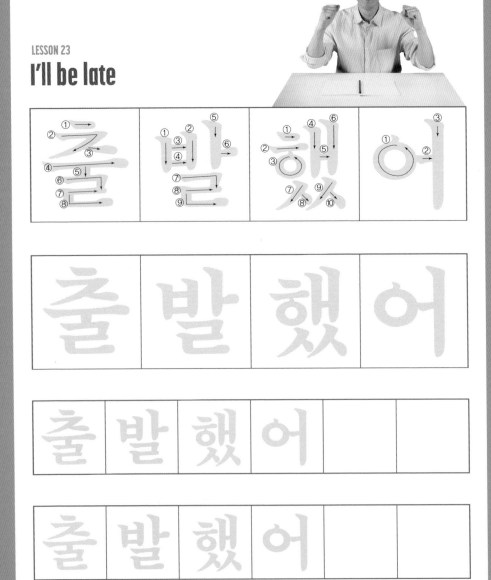

출	발	했	어		

출	발	했	어		

출	발	했	어		

출	발	했	어		

출	발	했	어		

출	발	했	어		

출	발	했	어		

What am I doing?

현타 온다

hyeonta   onda

[hyʌntʰa onda]

피식대학 유튜브 채널에서 강의 영상을 확인하세요.(추후 업로드 예정)
Please check the video of the lecture on our
YouTube channel of Psick University.(Uploading soon)

Kenneth 제가 게임에서 져서 그러는데…
Excuse me…

Jaesook 진지한 얘기 중이에요.
You're not my type.

Daniel 민수 오늘 너무 안된다. 그러지 말고 한 번만 더 가봐.
Kenneth… today is not your day. Hey come on,
hit her up one more time.

(5시간 후 5 hours later)

Kenneth 제가 게임에서 져서 그러는데…
Excuse me…

Regina 진지한 얘기 중이라고요.
What the… you're not my type.

Daniel 야 민수야, 밖에 해 떴어.
Hey Kenneth… the sun is up outside.

Kenneth 아… 현타 온다.
Ah…I am hyeonta onda.

Daniel 현타 온다.
What am I doing…

Kenneth 현타 온다…
What am I doing…

K&D 우리 현타 온다…
What are we doing…

Let's read and write

What am I doing?

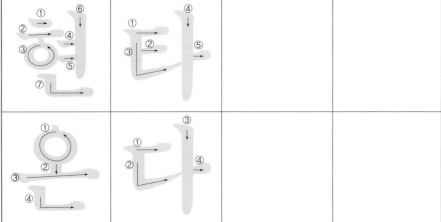

현	타		온	다	
현	타		온	다	
현	타		온	다	
현	타		온	다	
현	타		온	다	
현	타		온	다	
현	타		온	다	

I will never see you again

밥 한번 묵자

bap   hanbeon   mukja

[paρ hanpʌn muktša]

피식대학 유튜브 채널에서 강의 영상을 확인하세요.
Please check the video of the lecture on our
YouTube channel of Psick University.

Daniel 어… 야, 민… 수야…
Uh… hey Kenne… th…

Kenneth 어… 용주 형.
Uh… Daniel…

Daniel 어… 야 오랜만이다.
Hey… long… time no see.

Kenneth 어… 어… 잘 지냈어?
Yeah… you've been good?

Daniel 그… 뭐… 잘 지냈지…
Yeah yeah… I've been okay.

Kenneth 좋아 보인다.
You look good.

Daniel 어, 그래.
Thank you.

Kenneth 밥 한번 묵자.
We will bap hanbeon mukja.

Daniel 어, 그… 그래, 밥 한번 먹자.
Yes, I will never see you again.

K&D 우리 밥 한번 먹자!
We will never see each other again.

Let's read and write

I will never see you again

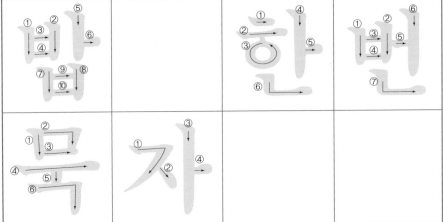

밥		한	번		묵
자					

밥		한	번		묵
자					

밥		한	번		묵
자					

밥		한	번		묵
자					

Unbelievable

이왜진?

iwaejin

[iwɛdzin]

피식대학 유튜브 채널에서 강의 영상을 확인하세요.
Please check the video of the lecture on our
YouTube channel of Psick University.

Kenneth 저기요, 그 코미디언 이용주 씨 맞으시죠?
Excuse me, you must be Daniel,
the famous comedian, right?

Daniel 사람 잘못 보셨습니다.
You got the wrong person.

Kenneth 아닌데? 이용주 맞는데?
No way, you must be Daniel yongju Lee!

Daniel 네, 맞습니다.
Yes, it's me.

Kenneth 이왜진?
Iwaejin?

Daniel 맞습니다.
Yes, I'm Daniel.

Kenneth 이왜진?
Unbelievable!

Daniel 진짭니다.
Yes, I am.

Kenneth 이왜진?!
Oh my god!
I can't believe it.

Let's read and write

LESSON 26
Unbelievable

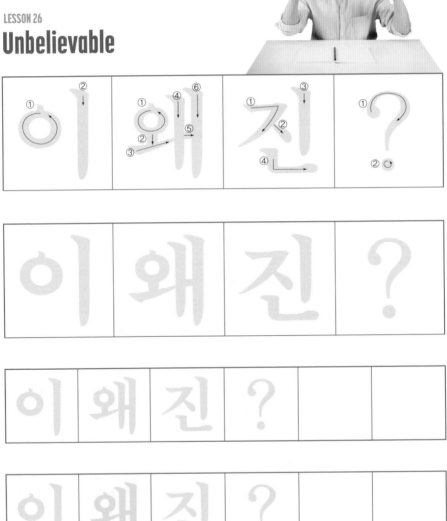

이 왜 진 ?

이 왜 진 ?

이 왜 진 ?

이	왜	진	?		
이	왜	진	?		
이	왜	진	?		
이	왜	진	?		
이	왜	진	?		
이	왜	진	?		
이	왜	진	?		

I might get wasted tonight

술이 단데?

suri   dande

[sʰuri tande]

피식대학 유튜브 채널에서 강의 영상을 확인하세요.(추후 업로드 예정)
Please check the video of the lecture on our
YouTube channel of Psick University.(Uploading soon)

Daniel	야, 민수야, 오늘 진짜 끝까지 가는 거야!
	Yo, Kenneth. You are getting wasted tonight.

Kenneth	아, 안 돼, 나 오늘 피곤해서 많이 못 마셔.
	No, man. I'm really tired.

Daniel	그러지 말고 오늘 밤새 놀아보자! 자 원샷!
	Come on. Let's party all night! Bottom's up!

Kenneth	어… 큰일 났다.
	Oh no…

Daniel	왜, 무슨 일이야?
	Why? What's up?

Kenneth	술이 단데?
	It is suri dande?

Daniel	뭐라고?!
	What did you say?

Kenneth	술이 단데?!
	I might get wasted tonight!

Daniel	오늘 제대로 날 잡았구나!
	Tonight is the night?

K&D	민수는 오늘 술이 단데?!
	Kenneth might get wasted tonight!

Let's read and write

I might get wasted tonight

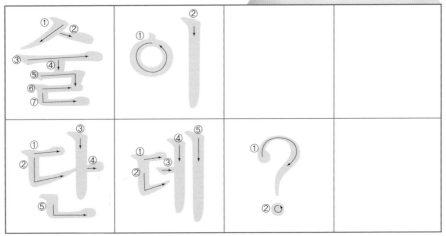

| 술 | 이 | | 단 | 데 | ? |

| 술 | 이 | | 단 | 데 | ? |

| 술 | 이 | | 단 | 데 | ? |

| 술 | 이 | | 단 | 데 | ? |

| 술 | 이 | | 단 | 데 | ? |

| 술 | 이 | | 단 | 데 | ? |

| 술 | 이 | | 단 | 데 | ? |

Just kidding

막 이래

mak   irae

[magirɛ]

피식대학 유튜브 채널에서 강의 영상을 확인하세요.(추후 업로드 예정)
Please check the video of the lecture on our
YouTube channel of Psick University.(Uploading soon)

Let's put it to use

Daisy
오늘 파티 물 진짜 좋다.
Damn, this party is on fire.

Katherine
그러게, 오늘 완전 할리우드다.
Yeah, so many hot guys!

Daisy
야야, 두 시, 두 시 방향, 저 남자 우리한테 온다.
Hey, 2 o'clock. He's coming to us.

Jaehyung
저기요, 귀여운 바비 누님들, 같이 놀래요?
Hello, cute lil barbies. Wanna party with us?

Katherine
바비요? 내가 바비보단 몸매 좋지 ㅋㅋㅋ 막 이래!
Barbie? I'm hotter than Barbie. Mak irae.

Jaehyung
…네?
Huh?

Daisy
내가 마고 로비 좀 닮긴 했어 ㅋㅋㅋ 막 이래!
People say I look like Margo Robbie. Just kidding!

Jaehyung
네…?
What the…

Katherine
여기서 우리가 제일 예쁘긴 해 ㅋㅋㅋ 막 이래!
We know we are the hottest here. Just kidding~

Jaehyung
(절레절레) 하… 쟤네 둘은 막 이래…
(Smh) Oh… what happened…

Let's read and write

Just kidding

29
LESSON

He is a red flag

믿거

mitgeo

[mitkʌ]

피식대학 유튜브 채널에서 강의 영상을 확인하세요.(추후 업로드 예정)
Please check the video of the lecture on our
YouTube channel of Psick University.(Uploading soon)

Daisy 야, 민순아.
Hey, Katherine!

Katherine 어, 용숙 언니!
Hi, Daisy!

Daisy 나 이번에 남소 받았어.
I'm going on a blind date.

Katherine 어떤데?
Any good?

Daisy 팔에 문신도 가득 있고 멋있어.
He's all tatted and cool.

Katherine 아… 그래? 옷은 잘 입어?
Oh… I see. Does he dress well?

Daisy 쫄티에 형광 반바지 입는데 너무 귀여워.
Tight shirts, neon shorts, so cute.

Katherine 문신 돼지네… 믿거!
Oh… He's a tattooed pig!
He is mitgeo.

Daisy 왜, 괜찮지 않아?
Oh come on, he is sexy.

Katherine 믿거!
He is a red flag.

LESSON 29   133

Let's read and write

He is a red flag

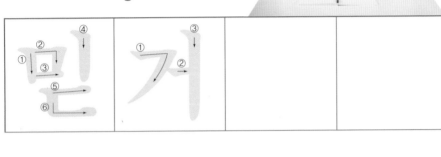

Let's make your situation

30
LESSON

It's not yours
돗대야
dotdaeya

[tot̚ɛ̃ya]

피식대학 유튜브 채널에서 강의 영상을 확인하세요.(추후 업로드 예정)
Please check the video of the lecture on our
YouTube channel of Psick University.(Uploading soon)

Daniel 아, 당 떨어진다. 뭐 먹을 거 없나?
I'm so tired. Do we have any snacks?

Kenneth (쩝쩝)
(Yum yum)

Daniel 야, 너 뭐 먹어?
Yo, Kenneth. What are you eating?

Kenneth 어? 이거 새콤달콤.
This is chewing jelly.

Daniel 나도 하나만 주라.
Can I have some?

Kenneth 아, 돛대야.
This is dotdaeya.

Daniel 그러지 말고 하나만 줘.
Come on. Give me one.

Kenneth 돛대야.
It's not yours.

Daniel 진짜 치사하게 그럴래?
Why you being so petty?

Kenneth 돛대야.
It's not yours.

Let's read and write

LESSON 30
It's not yours

돛	대	야			

돛	대	야			

돛	대	야			

돛	대	야			

돛	대	야			

돛	대	야			

돛	대	야			

Drinking Game Culture

1. You have to sing the intro.

2. You have to join even when you don't know how to play the game. (In Korea, you learn as you drink.)

3. You have to sing for the loser.

Intro song

Random game for ○○
○○(이)가 좋아하는 랜덤 게임, 무슨 게임

○○(i)ga joahaneun raendeom geim, museun geim

Game start, game start
게임 스타트, 게임 스타트

geim seutateu, geim seutateu

Drinking song

It's going in, drink, drink, drink, drink
마셔라, 마셔라, 마셔라, 마셔라

masyeora, masyeora, masyeora, masyeora

Going in, going in, going in, going in
술이 들어간다, 쭉쭉쭉쭉쭉, 쭉쭉쭉쭉쭉

suri deureoganda jjukjjukjjukjjukjjuk, jjukjjukjjukjjukjjuk

Don't let me wait around doing the shoulder dance
언제까지 어깨춤을 추게 할 거야

eonjekkaji eokkaechumeul chuge hal geoya

Look at my shoulders, they're dislocated!
내 어깨를 봐, 탈골됐잖아

nae eokkaereul bwa, talgoldwaetjana

Part 3

DATING/
ROMANCE
연애 생활

31
LESSON

I just want to fight you

나 뭐
na   mwo

달라진 거
dallajin   geo

없어?
eopseo

[na mwʌ talladzin kʌ ʌpsʌ] ·

피식대학 유튜브 채널에서 강의 영상을 확인하세요.(추후 업로드 예정)
Please check the video of the lecture on our
YouTube channel of Psick University.(Uploading soon)

Let's put it to use

Daniel 민순아!
Katherine!

Katherine 어! 용주 오빠!
Hey boo!

Daniel 우리 오랜만에 데이트인데 찐하게 놀자.
Let's have a lovely time today.

Katherine 나도 오빠 오랜만에 보니까 너무 좋다.
It's been so long. I missed you.

Daniel 사랑해, 민순아.
I love you, Kathy.

Katherine 응, 나도 오빠! 근데 나 뭐 달라진 거 없어?
Love you too. But, na mwo dallajin geo eopseo?

Daniel 어…?
Huh…?

Katherine 나 뭐 달라진 거 없냐구.
I just want to fight you.

Daniel 갑자기 왜 그래, 분위기 좋았잖아.
Come on, why you ruin the vibe.

Katherine 아니, 나 뭐 달라진 거 없어?
I just want to fight you!

Daniel 내가 다 잘못했어.
I don't know what I did, but I'm sorry…

Let's read and write

LESSON 31

I just want to fight you

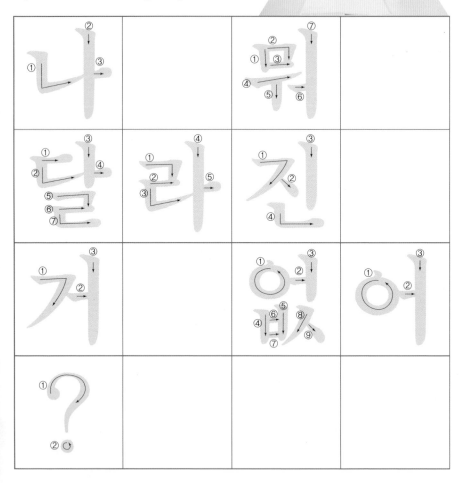

나   뭐

달   라   진

거   없   어

?

나		뭐		달	라
진		거		없	어
?					

나		뭐		달	라
진		거		없	어
?					

나		뭐		달	라
진		거		없	어
?					

I wanna date you

핸드크림

haendeukeurim

바를래?

bareullae

[hendukʰɯrim parullɛ]

피식대학 유튜브 채널에서 강의 영상을 확인하세요.(추후 업로드 예정)
Please check the video of the lecture on our
YouTube channel of Psick University.(Uploading soon)

(술 게임 하는 중 In a drinking game)

Kenneth   1번, 3번, 러브샷 해!
Number 1 and number 3, have a love shot!

(시끌벅적 Hullabaloo)

Daisy   재형 오빠, 진짜 오랜만이다!
Jaehyeong, it's been a while!

Jaehyung   진짜 오랜만이다, 우리 졸업하고 5년 만이네.
Yes, long time no see.
Maybe it's been five years since we graduated.

Daisy   아직 여자친구 없어?
Um··· don't you have a girlfriend yet?

Jaehyung   나 헤어졌어.
Actually··· I just broke up···

Daisy   핸드크림 바를래?
Haendeukeurim bareullae?

Jaehyung   핸드크림 바를래?
You wanna date me?

Daisy   핸드크림 바를래?!
I wanna date you!

Let's read and write

I wanna date you

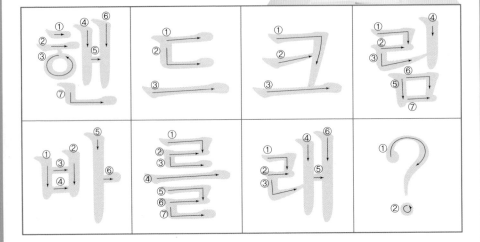

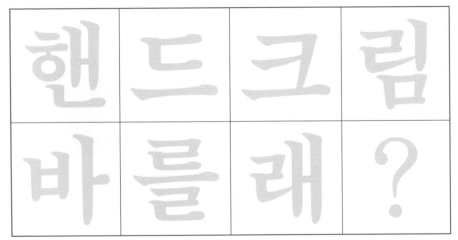

핸	드	크	림		바
를	래	?			

핸	드	크	림		바
를	래	?			

핸	드	크	림		바
를	래	?			

핸	드	크	림		바
를	래	?			

It's an announcement

너한테만
neohanteman

말하는 건데
malhaneun   geonde

[nʌhantʰeman malhanɯn gʌnde]

피식대학 유튜브 채널에서 강의 영상을 확인하세요.(추후 업로드 예정)
Please check the video of the lecture on our
YouTube channel of Psick University.(Uploading soon)

Let's put it to use

Daniel 자기야, 그거 들었어?

Hey baby, did you hear that?

Katherine 어 오빠, 아니, 못 들었어.

Oh Daniel, no, I didn't.

Daniel 그게 있잖아… 아, 아니다.

Actually… um… never mind.

Katherine 뭔데! 얼른 말해줘.

Hey, come on!

Daniel 너한테만 말하는 건데, 재혁이랑 인나랑 그렇고 그런 사이래.

This is neohanteman malhaneun geonde, Jaehyuk and Inna have something going on.

Katherine 진짜?

For real?

Daniel 이거 진짜 너한테만 말하는 건데, 재혁이 지금 바람피운대!

And it's an announcement, Jaehyuk is cheating on his girlfriend!

Katherine 세상에 이런 일이!

Unbelievable!

Daniel 이거 진짜 너한테만 말하는 건데!! (속닥속닥)

And it's another announcement… (whisper)

LESSON 33

It's an announcement

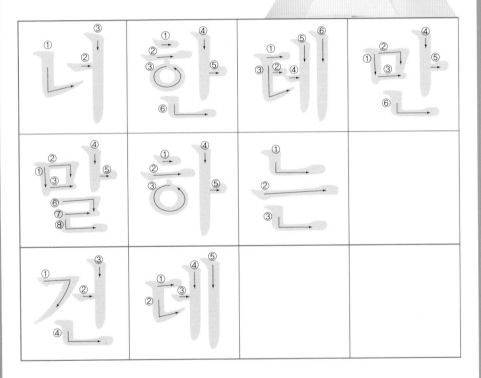

너한테만 말하는 건데

너한테만 말하는 건데

너한테만 말하는 건데

너한테만 말하는 건데

I'm not interested in you

아 진짜요?

a   jinjjayo

[a tsintsayo]

피식대학 유튜브 채널에서 강의 영상을 확인하세요.(추후 업로드 예정)
Please check the video of the lecture on our
YouTube channel of Psick University.(Uploading soon)

(소개팅 중 On a blind date)

Daniel 안녕하세요, 처음 뵙겠습니다, 이용주입니다.
Hi, nice to meet you, I'm Daniel.

Katherine 아, 네 안녕하세요, 김민순이에요.
Hi, I'm Katherine.

Daniel 간단히 저를 소개하자면, 제가 지금 차고 있는 시계는 5천만 원이고, 지난달에는 얼마 못 벌어서 3천만 원 벌었어요.
To introduce myself briefly, my watch is 50 million won, and I made 30 million won last month because it was a slow month.

Katherine 아 진짜요?
A jinjjayo?

Daniel 그리고 또, 또, 또 한강 보이는 50평 아파트에 살고 있어요.
And I live in a mansion with a view of the Han river.

Katherine 아 진짜요?
I'm not interested in you.

Daniel 아 그리고 또 저희 집안은 유ㅅ…
And then, my family has a long history…

Katherine 아… 진짜요?
I'm not interested in you!!!

Let's read and write

LESSON 34
I'm not interested in you

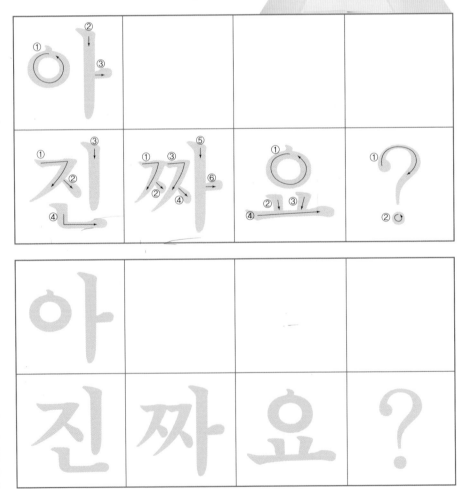

아

진짜요?

아

진짜요?

158   DAILY KOREAN

아		진	짜	요	?
아		진	짜	요	?
아		진	짜	요	?
아		진	짜	요	?
아		진	짜	요	?
아		진	짜	요	?
아		진	짜	요	?

I'm into you

메로나 먹으러

merona   meogeureo

갈래?

gallae

[merona mʌgɯrʌ kallɛ]

피식대학 유튜브 채널에서 강의 영상을 확인하세요. (추후 업로드 예정)
Please check the video of the lecture on our
YouTube channel of Psick University.(Uploading soon)

Let's put it to use

Daniel 민순아, 맛있게 먹고 있어?
Katherine, are you enjoying the meal?

Katherine 네 선배님, 챙겨주셔서 감사해요.
Yeah, thanks for taking care of me.

Daniel 취한 모습도 귀엽구나.
You look even cutter when you are drunk.

Katherine 아니에요.
Shut up⋯

Daniel 술도 깰 겸 우리⋯ 메로나 먹으러 갈래?
Let's get something to sober up, merona meogeureo gallae?

Katherine 네?
Huh?

Daniel 메로나 먹으러 갈래?
I'm into you.

Katherine 저 근데 남자친구 있는데⋯
I have a boyfriend.

Daniel 그러지 말고
우리 메로나 먹으러
갈래?
I'm into you!

Let's read and write

I'm into you

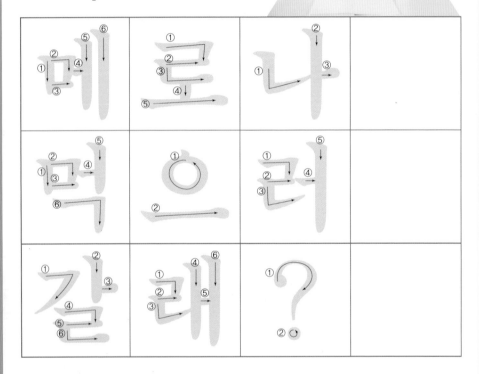

메로나 먹으러 갈래?

메로나 먹으러 갈래?

메로나 먹으러 갈래?

메로나 먹으러 갈래?

I miss you

자니?

jani

[tsaɲi]

피식대학 유튜브 채널에서 강의 영상을 확인하세요.(추후 업로드 예정)
Please check the video of the lecture on our
YouTube channel of Psick University.(Uploading soon)

Let's put it to use

(전 여자친구의 사진을 보며 Looking at ex-girlfriend's picture)

Kenneth   흑흑 흑흑
(Sobbing)

Kenneth   어떻게 하면 다시 만날 수 있을까?
How can I get back together with you…

Kenneth   나 아직 너를 많이 좋아해.
I still love you so much.

Kenneth   아, 이건 너무 찌질하다.
No, it sounds like a loser.

Kenneth   아무리 생각해도 내가 뭘 잘못했는지 모르겠어.
I don't really understand what I did wrong.

Kenneth   아… 이건 너무 공격적인가.
Hmm… does this sound aggressive?

Kenneth   아, 뭐라고 보내야 하지…?
Man, what should I say to her…

Kenneth   자니?
Jani?

Kenneth   자니?!
I miss you…

Kenneth   자니?!?!
I miss you…
Please comeback to me.

Let's read and write

I miss you

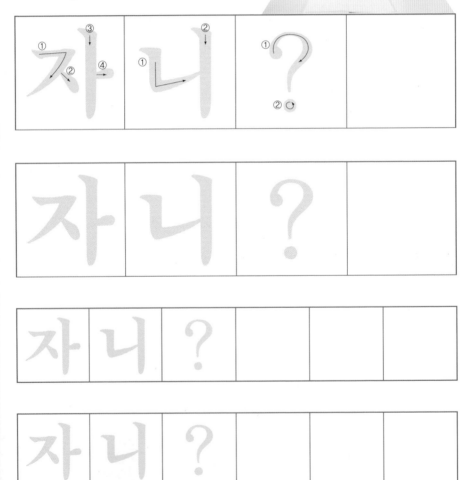

Let's make your situation

Your girlfriend is so hot

세금 더 내라

segeum   deo   naera

[sʰegɯm tʌ nɛra]

피식대학 유튜브 채널에서 강의 영상을 확인하세요.
Please check the video of the lecture on our
YouTube channel of Psick University.

Daniel	너 요즘 연애해?
	Are you dating anyone?

Kenneth	어떻게 알았어?!
	How did you know that?!

Daniel	이 녀석 입이 귀에 걸렸네.
	Your face says everything.

Kenneth	아 진짜?
	Ah, really?

Daniel	잔말 말고 사진 까봐.
	Cut the crap, and let me see her photo.

Kenneth	여기.
	Here.

Daniel	이야… 너 세금 더 내라.
	Wow… you must segeum deo naera.

Kenneth	세금 더 내라?
	Pretty, right?

Daniel	세금 더 내라!
	Your girlfriend is so hot!

Kenneth	세금 더 낼까?
	Right??

K&D	민수는 세금 더 내라.
	Kenneth must segeum deo naera.

Let's read and write

LESSON 37

Your girlfriend is so hot

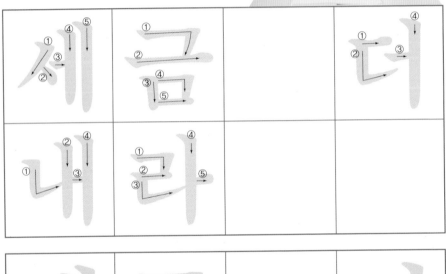

세금 더 내
라

세금 더 내
라

세금 더 내
라

세금 더 내
라

38
LESSON

I don't like your clothes
이 옷을 되게
i   oseul   doege
좋아하나 봐
joahana   bwa

[i osʰul twege dzoahana pwa]

피식대학 유튜브 채널에서 강의 영상을 확인하세요.
Please check the video of the lecture on our
YouTube channel of Psick University.

Katherine (통화 중) 어 오빠! 오늘 예쁘게 입고 와야 돼!
(On the phone) Hey, honey!
You have to dress up nicely today, alright?

Daniel 민순아! 나 오늘 멋있지?
Hey, Katherine! Look, don't I look good today?

Katherine 어… 오빠… 이 옷 또 입고 왔네…
Uh… honey… you're wearing this again…

Daniel 물론!
Of course I am!

Katherine 오빠는 이 옷을 되게 좋아하나 봐.
Honey, I think you i oseul doege joahana bwa.

Daniel 물론!
I do!

Katherine 이 옷을 되게 좋아하나 봐.
I don't like your clothes.

Daniel 물론이지.
Absolutely!

Katherine 오빠는!! 이 옷을 되게 좋아하나 봐!!
I hate your clothes!!

Let's read and write

LESSON 38
I don't like your clothes

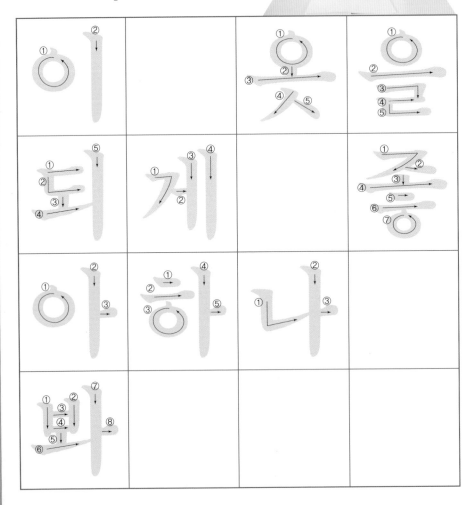

이　　옷을　　되게　　좋아하나봐

이　　옷을　　되게　　좋아하나봐

이　　옷을　　되게　　좋아하나봐

Excuse me?

제가 게임에서
jega   geimeseo

져서 그러는데
jyeoseo   geureoneunde

[tsega keimes^{h}ʌ tsʌs^{h}ʌ kɯrʌnɯnde]

피식대학 유튜브 채널에서 강의 영상을 확인하세요.
Please check the video of the lecture on our
YouTube channel of Psick University.

Kenneth   와, 여기 예쁜 여자들 진짜 많다.
Wow··· there are so many pretty girls around here!

Daniel   야, 야, 저기 봐봐, 두 시 방향.
여자 둘, 출동해, 빨리 가!
Hey, hey, over there, two o'clock.
You see two girls, right? You should go. Hurry up!

(여자들 쪽으로 접근하는 민수. Kenneth approaches a table of girls.)

Kenneth   제가 게임에서 져서 그러는데···
Jega geimeseo jyeoseo geureoneunde···

(혼자 돌아오는 민수. Kenneth comes back alone.)

Daniel   야 너 뭐야?
Hey, what was that?

Kenneth   진지한 얘기 중이라는데?
They said that I'm not their type.

Daniel   바보야 나와봐, 그것도 하나 제대로 못 해?
You stupid, get out of my way, you can't do anything right?

Daniel   제가 게임에서 져서 그러는데···
Excuse me?

(뺨 맞는 소리 Slap!)

K&D   우리가 게임에서
져서 그러는데···
We're playing dare
or truth···

Let's read and write

LESSON 39

Excuse me?

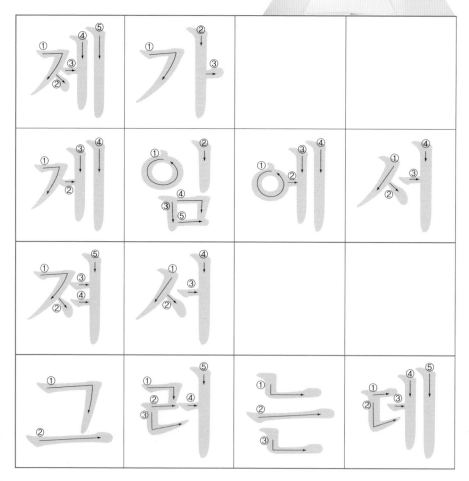

제가 게임에
서 져서 그
러는데

제가 게임에
서 져서 그
러는데

제가 게임에
서 져서 그
러는데

You're not my type

진지한 얘기
jinjihan   yaegi

중이에요
jungieyo

[tsindzihan yɛgi dzuɲieyo]

피식대학 유튜브 채널에서 강의 영상을 확인하세요.
Please check the video of the lecture on our
YouTube channel of Psick University.

Katherine   오늘 여기 있는 남자랑 다 키스해야지~
I'm going to kiss every single guy here tonight.

Daniel   헤이, 뜨거운 여자들~ 나랑 한잔할래?
Hey, hot ladies~ Do you want to have a drink with me?

Katherine   죄송합니다.
Sorry, we are busy.

Daniel   내가 한잔 살게.
Drink is on me!

Katherine   죄송합니다.
Sorry~

Daniel   너무 예뻐서 그래, 같이 한잔하자.
You are just my type. Come drink with me.

Katherine   진지한 얘기 중이에요.
We are having jinjihan yaegi jungieyo.

Daniel   뭐라고?
What?

Katherine   진지한 얘기 중이에요.
I'm sorry, you're not my type.

Daniel   뭐라고?
Are you serious?

Katherine   진지한 얘기 중이에요.
Yes, you're not my type.

Let's read and write

LESSON 40

You're not my type

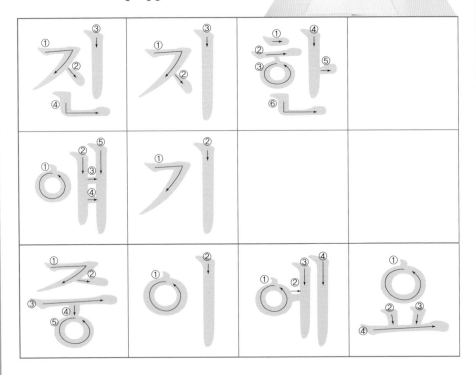

진지한 애기
중이에요

진지한 애기
중이에요

진지한 애기
중이에요

진지한 애기
중이에요

41
LESSON

Netflix and chill?

우리 집에
uri   jibe

고양이
goyangi

보러 갈래?
boreo   gallae

[uri tsibe koyaŋi porʌ kallɛ]

 피식대학 유튜브 채널에서 강의 영상을 확인하세요.(추후 업로드 예정)
Please check the video of the lecture on our
YouTube channel of Psick University.(Uploading soon)

Katherine   아, 왜 이렇게 취하지…
Oh, I feel so tipsy. I'm getting drunk.

Daniel   많이 힘들어?
Are you okay?

Katherine   오늘 좀 힘드네, 집에 가야겠다.
I got drunk so fast today. I should go home.

Daniel   저기… 우리 집에 고양이 보러 갈래?
Uhm… uri jibe goyangi boreo gallae?

Katherine   헐 진짜?! 고양이 키워?
Really? You got a Netflix ID?

Daniel   우리 집에 고양이 보러 갈래?
You wanna Netflix and chill?

Katherine   그냥 사진으로 보여줘.
I just want to watch here.

Daniel   우리 집에 고양이 보러 갈래??
I wanna Netflix and chill with you.

Let's read and write

Netflix and chill?

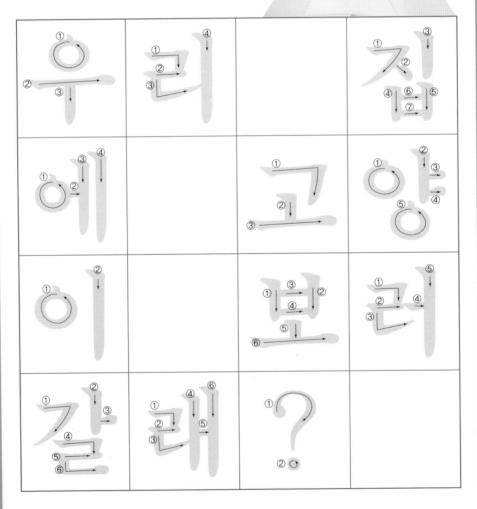

우	리		집	에	
고	양	이		보	러
갈	래	?			

우	리		집	에	
고	양	이		보	러
갈	래	?			

우	리		집	에	
고	양	이		보	러
갈	래	?			

Smoking Etiquette

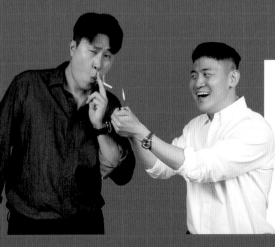

How to use a lighter

1. Make sure the flame isn't too big because it might offend the smoker.

2. Cover wind with one hand and make a flame with the other hand.

How to smoke a cigar

1. Turn your head, cover your cigarette, then inhale.

2. Blow out the smoke downwards and wave to quickly remove the smoke.

- Conversation happens when people smoke together.

- Koreans share their thoughts and deep conversations they don't usually share when they smoke together.

- If you want to be close to someone, go out with the person when s/he goes out to have a smoke.

- Koreans don't like smokers.

- People will throw you a dirty look if you smoke walking on the street.

Part 4

AT WORK
직장 생활

He is useless

애는 착해

aeneun   chakae

[ɛnɯn tsʰakʰɛ]

피식대학 유튜브 채널에서 강의 영상을 확인하세요.
Please check the video of the lecture on our
YouTube channel of Psick University.

Let's put it to use

Kenneth 하… 도대체 왜 일을 이렇게 해놓은 거야?
How could this fool do such an awful job?

Daniel 어, 김 대리.
Hey, Kenneth.

Kenneth 네, 부장님.
Oh, Daniel.

Daniel 이번에 새로 들어온 인턴은 어떻게, 일 잘해?
Is the new intern working with you doing a good job?

Kenneth 어… 쩝, 아닙니다.
Uhm… yeah… sort of.

Daniel 아이, 그러지 말고 얘기해 봐. 일 잘해?
Hey, come on, talk to me. Is he doing a good job?

Kenneth 아니 제가 3일 동안 같이 해봤는데요… 애는 착해요.
I've been working with him for three days, and… aeneun chakaeyo.

Daniel 아니, 일을 잘하냐고.
No, I mean… how is he doing?

Kenneth 그러니까, 애는 착해요.
It's like, he's a good kid.

Daniel 아니, 일을 잘하냐니까?
Jesus Christ… is he any good?

Kenneth 그러니까, 애는 착해요.
So, he is useless!

LESSON 42

He is useless

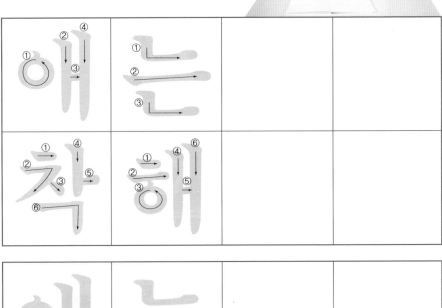

애	는		착	해	
애	는		착	해	
애	는		착	해	
애	는		착	해	
애	는		착	해	
애	는		착	해	
애	는		착	해	

I can't do that

넵

nep

[nep]

피식대학 유튜브 채널에서 강의 영상을 확인하세요.(추후 업로드 예정)
Please check the video of the lecture on our
YouTube channel of Psick University.(Uploading soon)

Let's put it to use

Daniel	어이, 김 대리, 많이 바빠? Hey Kenneth, are you busy?
Kenneth	부장님! 괜찮습니다. Hi Daniel, no I'm not.
Daniel	다른 건 아니고, 내가 내일 휴가인데 보고서 좀 써줄 수 있어? Actually, I'll be on my vacation starting tomorrow. So can you write a report for me?
Kenneth	그… 제가 내일까지 기획안을 내야 하는데… Um… I have a lot to do by tomorrow…
Daniel	그러지 말고 서로 상부상조하자. You'll scratch my back and I'll scratch your back.
Kenneth	…넵. Nep.
Daniel	가능한 거지? You can do that?
Kenneth	넵. I can't do that.
Daniel	괜찮은 거지? We're good, right?
Kenneth	넵. Yes.

Let's read and write

I can't do that

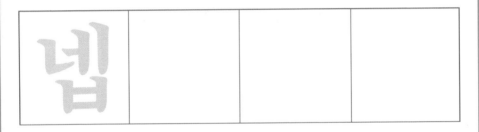

Let's make your situation

You're gonna be canceled

너 말 나와

neo   mal   nawa

[nʌ mal nawa]

피식대학 유튜브 채널에서 강의 영상을 확인하세요.(추후 업로드 예정)
Please check the video of the lecture on our
YouTube channel of Psick University.(Uploading soon)

Let's put it to use

Daniel	김 대리, 나랑 잠깐 얘기 좀 할까? Kenneth, can we have a talk?
Kenneth	네 부장님. Yes, sir.
Daniel	너 나랑 둘만 있을 때 반말하는 건 괜찮은데, 다른 데서 그러면 안 돼. It's okay to talk to me casually in private but you should be formal to me in public.
Kenneth	에이 형, 뭐 어때요, 원래 알던 사인데. Come on bro. We've been friends for long. Who cares?
Daniel	민수야, 너 말 나와. Hey, Kenneth! Neo mal nawa.
Kenneth	나 말 나와? I'm gonna be canceled?
Daniel	어, 너 말 나와! Yes, you're gonna be canceled!
K&D	민수는 말 나와! Kenneth is gonna be canceled!

Let's read and write

LESSON 44

You're gonna be canceled

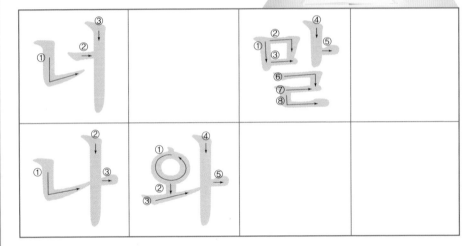

너		말		나	와
너		말		나	와
너		말		나	와
너		말		나	와
너		말		나	와
너		말		나	와
너		말		나	와

I'm out

조장 하실 분?

jojang   hasil   bun

[tsodzaŋ haçil pun]

피식대학 유튜브 채널에서 강의 영상을 확인하세요. (추후 업로드 예정)
Please check the video of the lecture on our
YouTube channel of Psick University.(Uploading soon)

Let's put it to use

Kenneth 안녕하세요, 김민수입니다. 잘 부탁드립니다.
먼저 몇 가지 말씀드릴게요. 제가 맘이 여려서요,
말투 부드럽게 해주시고요. 여자친구가 질투하니까
여자분들은 개인 카톡 자제 부탁드려요.
Hello, everyone. I'm Kenneth. Pleasure to meet you guys.
Before we start, I have to ask you guys favors. I am very
sensitive so please be polite and my girlfriend is very jealous
so please don't send me personal Kakao talk messages.

Daniel 아… 네;;; 잘 부탁드려요.
Okay… welcome.

Kenneth 그리고 저 이번에 장학금 받아야 하니까 좋은 결과
만들어봐요.
And I have to get a scholarship so let's do our best!

Daniel 네, 좋아요.
Yeah, sure.

Kenneth 그러면, 조장 하실 분?
So, jojang hasil bun?

Daniel 네?
Huh?

Kenneth 조장 하실 분?
I'm out!

Daniel 뭐라고요?
What the?

Kenneth 조장 하실 분!!
I'm out!!!

Let's read and write

I'm out

죠	장		
하	실		
뿐	?		

조	장		하	실	
분	?				

조	장		하	실	
분	?				

조	장		하	실	
분	?				

조	장		하	실	
분	?				

Focus on your work

편해?

pyeonhae

[pʰyʌnhɛ]

피식대학 유튜브 채널에서 강의 영상을 확인하세요.
Please check the video of the lecture on our
YouTube channel of Psick University.

Daniel   김 대리, 다음 주 연차를 4일 붙여 쓰던데? 어제 퇴근은 몇 시에 했어?
Hey, Kenneth, you're using your annual leave for four days back to back, aren't you? What time did you get off work yesterday?

Kenneth   네, 그렇습니다. 어제 정시 퇴근 했습니다.
Yes··· I got off work on time yesterday.

Daniel   내가 들어보니까 요즘 사내 연애도 한다던데?
As far as I know, you're dating someone in the office, right?

Kenneth   그렇습니다, 사내 연애도 하고 있습니다.
Yes, I am. I'm in an office relationship.

Daniel   김 대리 요새 편해?
Hey Kenneth, are you pyeonhae in these day?

Kenneth   예? 아닙니다.
Sorry? I just···

Daniel   불편해?
Do you have trouble focusing on your work?

Kenneth   예? 아, 아니요.
No, I'm doing my best.

Daniel   편해?
Focus on your work!

Kenneth   예···?
But I'm···

Daniel   민수는 편해!!
Kenneth has to focus on his work!

Let's read and write

LESSON 46
Focus on your work

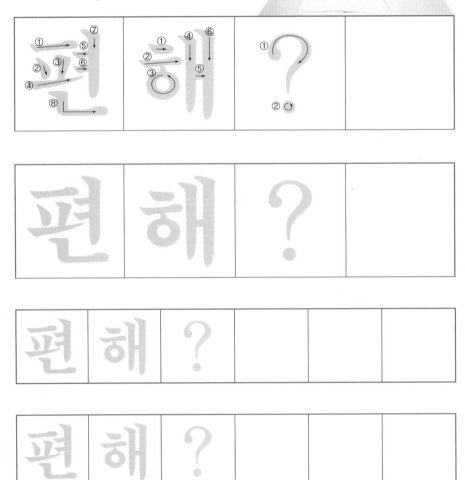

Let's make your situation

_____

_____

_____

_____

_____

_____

_____

_____

_____

_____

They are messing around

관리 안 하냐?

gwalli　　　an　　　hanya

[kwaʎʎi an haɲya]

피식대학 유튜브 채널에서 강의 영상을 확인하세요.(추후 업로드 예정)
Please check the video of the lecture on our
YouTube channel of Psick University.(Uploading soon)

Daniel 야 김 대리, 어제 정 사원이 나보다 먼저 퇴근하더라?
Hey Kenneth, Jeong left work before me, yesterday.

Kenneth 아… 정말입니까…?
Oh… really?

Daniel 나 때는 그런 거 상상도 못 했어.
When I was your age, I never even thought of going home before my boss did.

Kenneth 알고 있습니다.
I know that.

Daniel 야 김 대리, 관리 안 하냐?
Hey Kenneth, gwalli an hanya?

Kenneth 네…?
Sorry…?

Daniel 관리 안 하냐?
They are messing around.

Kenneth 그게 아니고…
Actually…

Daniel 관리 안 하냐?
They are messing around!

Let's read and write

They are messing around

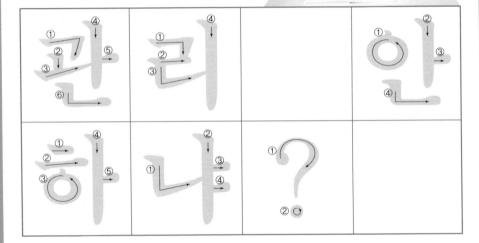

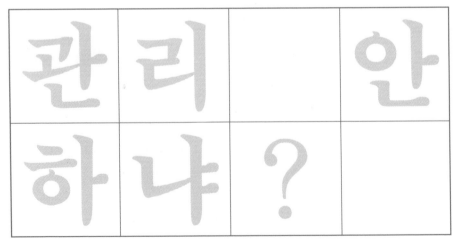

관	리		안		하
냐	?				

관	리		안		하
냐	?				

관	리		안		하
냐	?				

관	리		안		하
냐	?				

48
LESSON

Listen carefully

이 말까진

i　　　　　malkkajin

안 하려고

an　　　　haryeogo

했는데

haenneunde

[i malˈkadʑin an haryʌgo hɛnnɯnde]

피식대학 유튜브 채널에서 강의 영상을 확인하세요. (추후 업로드 예정)
Please check the video of the lecture on our
YouTube channel of Psick University.(Uploading soon)

Daniel

김 대리, 어제 회식 몇 차까지 갔어?

Hey Kenneth, how many rounds did you go to last night?

Kenneth

1차 하고 집에 갔습니다.

I went home after the first round.

Daniel

그럼 부장님 안 챙긴 거야?

So, you didn't take care of the manager, right?

Kenneth

그… 그렇습니다.

Yes…

Daniel

이 말까진 안 하려고 했는데, 사내 연애 하지 마.

I malkkajin an haryeogo haenneunde, don't date in the office.

Kenneth

죄송합니다.

I'm sorry…

Daniel

이 말까진 안 하려고 했는데, 출근은 10분 전까지 오는 거야.

Hey, listen carefully, basically you have to get to the office 10 minutes earlier, right?

Kenneth

죄송합니다.

Sorry…

Daniel

내가 이 말까진 진짜 안 하려고 했는데…

Listen carefully… and…

LESSON 48
Listen carefully

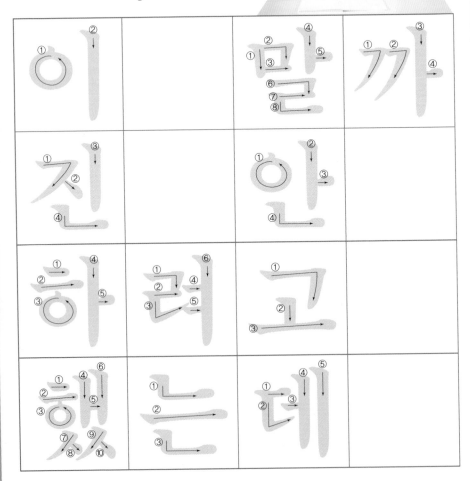

이		말	까
진		안	
하	려	고	
했	는	데	

이		말	까	진	
안		하	려	고	
했	는	데			

이		말	까	진	
안		하	려	고	
했	는	데			

이		말	까	진	
안		하	려	고	
했	는	데			

I'm gonna kill you

잠깐
jamkkan

시간 좀
sigan   jom

있어?
isseo

[tsamk̃an ɕigan tsom iˢʌ]

피식대학 유튜브 채널에서 강의 영상을 확인하세요.(추후 업로드 예정)
Please check the video of the lecture on our
YouTube channel of Psick University.(Uploading soon)

Jaehyung   김 대리님, 큰일입니다.
Kenneth, we got a problem.

Kenneth   어 그래, 정 인턴. 무슨 일이야?
What's the matter?

Jaehyung   어제 법카로 술 마신 거 부장님이 안 것 같습니다.
I think the manager found out that you paid for the drinks with the corporate card yesterday.

Kenneth   에이, 됐어. 그 양반 바보라 몰라…
Don't worry, he's a fool. He'll never know.

Daniel   어이, 김 대리.
Hey, Kenneth.

Kenneth   네, 부장님!
Oh! Daniel.

Daniel   잠깐 시간 좀 있어?
Jamkkan sigan jom isseo?

Kenneth   왜 그러시죠?
What's up?

Daniel   잠깐 시간 좀 있어?
I'm gonna kill you.

Kenneth   저 지금 바쁜데…
I don't understand…

Daniel   잠깐 시간 좀 있어?
I'm gonna kill you.

Let's read and write

LESSON 49

I'm gonna kill you

잠	깐		
시	간		
좀			
있	어	?	

잠깐 시간 좀 있어?

잠깐 시간 좀 있어?

잠깐 시간 좀 있어?

잠깐 시간 좀 있어?

50
LESSON

I beg your pardon?

잘 못
jal   mot

들었습니다?
deureotseumnida

[tsal mot ɨɯɾʌtsɨumɲida]

피식대학 유튜브 채널에서 강의 영상을 확인하세요.
Please check the video of the lecture on our
YouTube channel of Psick University.

Let's put it to use

(따르르릉, 따르르릉 RRRRR, RRRRR)

Jaehyung 네, 여보세요.
Hello?

Daniel 안녕하세요, 정재형 씨 맞으시죠?
Hi, is this Jeong Jaehyung speaking right now?

Jaehyung 예, 어디세요?
Yeah, this is Jeong Jaehyung. Who is it?

Daniel 여기 병무청입니다.
This is Military Manpower Administration.

Jaehyung 잘 못 들었습니다?
Jal mot deureotseumnida?

Daniel 병무청입니다.
This is Military Manpower Administration.

Jaehyung 잘 못 들었습니다…?
I beg your pardon…?

Daniel 병무청이라고요.
Don't make me say it again.

Jaehyung 나는 잘 못 들었습니다.
This can't be happening.

Let's read and write

LESSON 50

I beg your pardon?

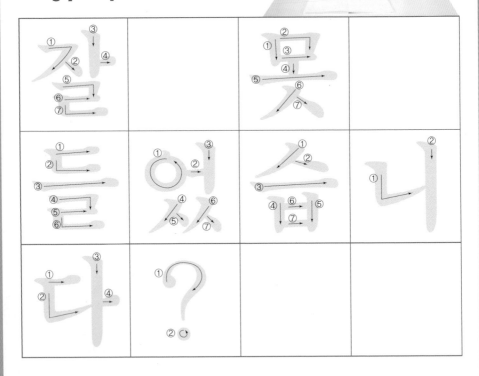

잘		못		들	었
습	니	다	?		

잘		못		들	었
습	니	다	?		

잘		못		들	었
습	니	다	?		

잘		못		들	었
습	니	다	?		

Something + 각

means be ready, poised to do something

Let's try it out

퇴사각 toesagak [tʰwesʰagaĸ]: poised to leave company

고소각 gosogak [kosʰogaĸ]: ready to sue

현피각 hyeonpigak [hyʌnpʰigaĸ]: ready to meet and fight

Wrap up! ⟩ **Quiz.**

Q. Which of the following words is awkward when used with '~gak'?

    a. 이별 breakup   b. 맛있다 be delicious
    c. 치킨 chicken   d. 칼퇴 leaving work on time

answer: b

02

~마렵다 maryeopda[maryʌp̚t̚a]

Something+마렵다

means you want to do something

Let's try it out

치킨 마렵다 chicken maryeopda[tʃʰɪkən maryʌp̚t̚a]: want chicken

딱밤 마렵다 ttakbam maryeopda[t̚ak̚p̚am maryʌp̚t̚a]: want to give a noogie

연애 마렵다 yeonae maryeopda[yʌnɛ maryʌp̚t̚a]: want to have a date

Wrap up! ▷ Quiz.

Q. Which of the following words is awkward when used with '~maryeopda'?

a. 동사무소 community service center
b. 마라탕 malatang
c. 맥주 beer
d. 싸대기 slap

answer: a

~특 teuk[tʰɯk̚]

Something (someone)+특

means a special trait of something/someone

Let's try it out

한국사람 특 hanguksaram teuk[hanguk̚s'aram tʰɯk̚]: a trait of Korean people

남자친구 특 namjachingu teuk[namdzatsʰingu tʰɯk̚]: a trait of a boyfriend

하남자 특 hanamja teuk[hanamdza tʰɯk̚]: a trait of a jerk

Wrap up! ▷ **Quiz.**

Q. Which of the following words is awkward when used with '~teuk'?

a. 옛날 사람 old man   b. 어쨌든 anyway

c. 외국인 foreigner   d. 여자친구 girlfriend

answer: b

04

～무새 musae[musʰɛ]

Something+무새

means someone who's obessed with something

Let's try it out

국밥무새 **gukbap**musae[kukp̀ap̀musʰɛ]: obsessed with gukbap(hot soup with rice)

백숙무새 **baeksuk**musae[pɛk̇ṡuk̇musʰɛ]: obsessed with baeksuk(chicken soup)

돈무새 **don**musae[tonmusʰɛ]: obsessed with money

Wrap up!　　Quiz.

Q. **Which of the following words is awkward when used with '~musae'?**

a. 넵 yes　　　　　　b. 술 drinking
c. 껄 should have　　d. 맡다 smell

answer: d

05

～알못 almot[almot]

Something+알못

means someone doesn't know well about something

Let's try it out

축 알못 chuk almot[tsʰuk almot]: don't know well about soccer

술 알못 sul almot[sʰul almot]: don't know well about alcohol(drink)

겜 알못 gem almot[kem almot]: don't know well about game

Wrap up! > **Quiz.**

Q. Which of the following words is awkward when used with '~almot'?

a. 농구 basketball   b. 차 car
c. 때문에 because   d. 영화 movie

answer: c

06

혼~ hon[hon]

혼+Something

means doing something alone

Let's try it out

혼**밥** hon**bap**[honp͈ap̚]: eat alone

혼**술** hon**sul**[honsʰul]: drink alone

혼**영** hon**yeong**[hoɲyʌŋ]: watch a movie alone

Wrap up!	Quiz.

Q. Which of the following words is awkward when used with 'hon~'?

a. 코노 coin karaoke
c. 공(부) study

b. (여)행 travel
d. 독재 dictatorship

answer: d

07

갑분~ gapbun[kap͈un]

갑분+Something

means that something is happening out of the blue

Let's try it out

갑분**싸** gapbun**ssa**[kap͈unśa]: suddenly get awkward

갑분**술** gapbun**sul**[kap͈unsʰul]: suddenly feel like drinking

갑분**치킨** gapbun**chicken**[kap͈untsʰikʰin]: suddenly want chicken

Wrap up! ⟩ **Quiz.**

Q. Which of the following words is awkward when used with 'gapbun~'?

a. 핫 hot

b. 싸지르다 take a piss

c. 로맨스 romance

d. 띠용 whoof

answer: b

억~ eok[ʌk̚]

억+Something

means doing something by force

Let's try it out

억텐 **eokten**[ʌk̚tʰen]: pretend to be excited, force someone to get excited

억까 **eokkka**[ʌk̚k̚a]: blame someone who did nothing wrong

억빠 **eokppa**[ʌk̚p̚a]: advocate someone no matter what

Wrap up!	Quiz.

Q. Which of the following Korean words does 'eok~' come from?

a. 억만장자 billionaire   b. 억누르다 suppress

c. 억지로 unwillingly be forced   d. 억수 downpour

answer: c

어쩔~ eojjeol[ʌtɕʌl]

어쩔+Something

means whatever

Let's try it out

어쩔 티비 eojjeol tibi[ʌtɕʌl tʰibi]: whatever TV

어쩔 냉장고 eojjeol naengjanggo[ʌtɕʌl nɛŋdzaŋgo]: whatever refrigerator

어쩔 스타일러 eojjeol styler[ʌtɕʌl stáilər]: whatever styler(electronic closet)

Wrap up! 〉 **Quiz.**

Q. Which of the following words is awkward when used with 'eojjeol~'?

a. 컴퓨터 computer   b. 긁기 scratching

c. 시크릿 쥬쥬 리미티드 에디션 Secret Juoju limited edition

answer: b

갓~, ~갓 gat[kaⱦ]

갓 + Something(someone), Something(someone) + 갓

means something(someone) is top-notch

Let's try it out

갓연아 gatYuna[kaⱦyʌna]: queen (Kim) Yuna

홍민갓 HeungMingat [huŋminkaⱦ]: (Son) Heungmin is king

갓겜 gatgem[kaⱦkem]: the game is top-notch

Wrap up!	Quiz.

Q. **Which of the following English words does 'gat' come from?**

   a. god   b. got
   c. cut   d. g.o.a.t

answer: a

In **English**	In **Korean**
Let's do it	ㄱㄱ
Yes	ㅇㅇ
No	ㄴㄴ
LOL	ㅋㅋ
Get out of	ㄲㅈ
Nope	ㅅㄹ
Where are you	ㅇㄷ
Shut up	ㄷㅊ
Really?	ㄹㅇ?
Hi	ㅎㅇ
Bye	ㅃㅇ

In **English**	In **Korean**
OMG···	ㄷㄷ
Tsk tsk	ㅉㅉ
Just wait	ㄱㄷ
Bye, keep working	ㅅㄱ
I'm sorry	ㅈㅅ
I agree	ㅇㅈ
Oh yeah!	ㄱㅇㄷ
Haha	ㅎㅎ
Thank you	ㄱㅅ
I don't know	ㅁㄹ
Congrat!	ㅊㅋ

DAILY
KOREAN

Cast

김민수
이용주
정재형

Producer

김세훈
김진현
박지훈
오세형
최현준

Creative

김상엽
김성구

Translation

이정빈

Production

피식대학
메타코미디

Special thanks

Deft (김혁규)
PSY (싸이)
Sonny (손흥민)
레오제이
폭스클럽